PRAISE FOR PIDGY!

"Written and fantastically illustrated by famed equine artist Jeanne Mellin, this re-release of a popular story from the 1950's offers a heartfelt story of a young girl and her discovery of the path of her dreams. Whether a horse enthusiast or not, this book is a loving, kind story with a huge amount of heart. Not to mention the gorgeous illustrations are something that both children and adults will absolutely love. Enjoy!"

—Amy Lignor,
BookPleasures.com

"*Pidgy's Surprise* addresses a situation that plays out in most homes, whether the object of the child's longing is a horse or not. Kids will immediately identify with Cindy, knowing how it feels to want something so badly and to have parents who just don't seem to understand. Author Jeanne Mellin allows young readers to think more deeply about the issues involved as they follow the story of Cindy and Pidgy, her Shetland pony. Quill says: Animal-lovers will enjoy the close relationship between a girl and her pony while learning to appreciate what they already have."

—Eloise Michael,
Feathered Quill Book Reviews

"The simple, graceful flow of the tale was charming and elegantly nostalgic while the phenomenal illustrations which liberally grace the pages of this book will satisfy the imagination of any horse-crazy youngster. If you loved Misty, Blaze, or Black Beauty, you're certain to find a place in your heart for Pidgy, a pudgy pony you're sure to fall in love with!"

—Deb Fowler,
Amazon Top 50 Reviewer

"I liked *Pidgy's Surprise* a lot. I really like horses and every time I see a horse I wish I could ride one. This story will teach you a lot about horses and how they can act and how you can train them. Kids of all ages would love to read this book to hear the loving story of Pidgy and Cindy."

—Madeline McElroy (age 9) for
Reader Views

D1399396

Pidgy's Surprise

THE MORGAN HORSE SERIES
BY ELLEN F. FELD
Read Them All!

Blackjack: Dreaming of a Morgan Horse

ISBN 978-0-9709002-8-9

An International Reading Association— Children's Book Council "Children's Choices" Selection

"Mrs. Feld has a true gift in capturing the imagination and engaging the reader. It isn't always easy to find a book that will be read willingly by pre-teens! Kudos to Mrs. Feld on her delightful *Morgan Horse* series."

— Jenefer Igarashi, Senior Editor,
   The Old Schoolhouse Magazine

Frosty: The Adventures of a Morgan Horse

ISBN 978-0-9831138-6-7

An International Reading Association— Children's Book Council "Children's Choices" Selection

"... a thoroughly delightful novel for young readers about a girl and her relationship with powerful and noble animals ... Frosty is a story to be cherished by horse lovers of all ages."

—*Midwest Book Review*

Rusty: The High-Flying Morgan Horse

ISBN 978-0-9831138-2-9

A Parent to Parent Adding Wisdom Award Winner

"Through her choice words and obvious first-hand knowledge, Ellen Feld conveys to the reader that special connection a girl has with her horse. A thoroughly enjoyable read—I only wish it had been published when I was a teenager!"

—Cindy Mark, Editor, *Horses All*

Robin: The Lovable Morgan Horse

ISBN 978-0-9709002-5-8

A Parent to Parent Adding Wisdom Award Winner

"Feld uses plenty of conflict on many levels, a string of obstacles, and the characters' solutions to craft a very interesting story with a quick pace. We rated this book five hearts."

—Bob Spear, *Heartland Reviews*

Annie: The Mysterious Morgan Horse

ISBN 978-0-9709002-9-6

A Moonbeam Children's Book Award Winner and A Reader Views Literary Award Winner

"Annie combines an exciting story with a lot of practical information. It's another blue-ribbon winner from author Ellen Feld!"

—*Horsemen's Yankee Pedlar*

Rimfire: The Barrel Racing Morgan Horse

ISBN 978-0-9709002-1-0

Selected as the Best New Book for 2010 by Tack 'n Togs Magazine

"Rimfire brings the exciting world of barrel racing to life in a fun and delightful way! A great book for our youth and a valuable reminder that quitters never win and winners never quit."

—Martha Josey, AQHA, WPRA, NBHA World Champion, Olympic Medalist, Hall of Fame

The Further Adventures of Blackjack: The Champion Morgan Horse

ISBN 978-0-9831138-5-0

The Further Adventures of Blackjack "... has excitement, suspense, and a surprise ending, all coming together with a satisfying understanding of horses. It is another blue-ribbon winner from a talented author."

—Nancy Norton, Editor,
Horse & Academy Magazine

Meet the Morgans

ISBN 978-0-9831138-4-3

The perfect companion book to the popular *Morgan Horse* series. With over 50 photos of the real horses behind the books, readers will get an inside look at the Morgans who inspired the series.

ALSO FROM WILLOW BEND PUBLISHING

Blackjack: The Magical Morgan Horse

ISBN: 978-0-9831138-6-7

A girl, a horse, and some magical stardust - sometimes dreams really do come true...

Shadow: The Curious Morgan Horse

ISBN 978-0-9831138-3-6

A USA Book News Best Books Award Winner

"You are guaranteed to delight in this story of a young, adventurous foal. Feld is a talented, creative, artistic writer who clearly loves her topic of horses. Absolutely delightful!"

—Viviane Crystal, *Crystal Reviews*

Justin Morgan and the Big Horse Race

ISBN 978-0-9831138-1-2

"A beautiful story with magnificent drawings that's pure entertainment."

—Amy Lignor, *Feathered Quill Book Reviews*

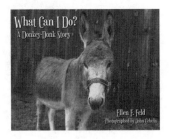

What Can I Do?
A Donkey-Donk Story

ISBN: 978-0-9831138-7-4

"If you are searching for a picture book to read to your homeschooler or class that will illicit smiles, peels of laughter, and giggles, then look no further."

—*Valerie Schuetta, M.Ed.,*
Classroom Reviews

What Does A Police Horse Do?

ISBN 978-0-9831138-9-8

Meet Liam - a police horse with the Lancaster, PA Mounted Police Unit. Follow along with this very special horse to learn just what a police horse does every day.

Pidgy's Surprise

Jeanne Mellin

Willow Bend Publishing
Goshen, Massachusetts

The publisher and author would like to acknowledge the hard work of Linda Mahoney of LM Design. Without Linda's tireless efforts to restore the text and original drawings, *Pidgy's Surprise* would have never come back to life.

Published by Willow Bend Publishing

Cover design and illustrations by Jeanne Mellin
Book design and typesetting by Linda Mahoney, LM Design

Library of Congress Control Number: 2011920625
ISBN: 978-0-9831138-0-5

Direct inquiries to:
Willow Bend Publishing
P.O. Box 304
Goshen, MA 01032
www.willowbendpublishing.com

Printed in the United States of America

10 9 8 7 6 5 4 3 2

To Tori —

Paint brushes and horses, always

Love, Nina

U U U

A NOTE TO READERS

Pidgy's Surprise was originally published in 1955, a time when safety helmets for riders were uncommon. Therefore, very few riders portrayed in the drawings are wearing helmets. However, both the publisher and author strongly urge every rider to use a certified equestrian helmet whenever mounted on a horse or pony.

DAYDREAMING

Cindy Sawyer sat on the split rail fence of the pasture. Sadly, she watched a small Shetland mare cropping the tender spring grass. The pony still had most of her long winter coat. She looked almost like a very woolly teddy bear except for her heavy mane and tail. She had begun to shed. Patches of short summer coat were showing through on her shoulders and flanks, giving her a raggedy, nobody-loves-me appearance. Cindy sighed. It wasn't that she didn't love the pony but she just wished the little mare weren't so plain. Besides her rough coat and fuzzy mane, she was a peculiar color, too: sort of a dark chestnut but not quite. Sometimes she looked almost dun. Sometimes she was just brown—a dull, reddish, unlovely brown.

The pony's name was Pigeon but everyone called her Pidgy. Poor Pidgy. No one ever said, "Look at the pretty pony," or, "Gee, Cindy, I wish I had a pony like Pidgy." All anyone seemed to say about her was, "My, isn't she fat," or, "How do you ever get the tangles out of that mane," or "Isn't she a funny color!" Cindy would listen to all the things people said about little Pidgy and pat the pony mournfully and wish that Pidgy were a horse.

This was Cindy Sawyer's dream: a horse, a big spirited horse like Pete Greene's Thoroughbred or even a middle-sized spirited horse like Shaw's Arabian. It didn't matter, really, as long as it had fire and vigor and was very beautiful. This morning Cindy had ridden Pigeon around the town for an hour or so pretending she was riding Shaw's Arabian. With her heels nudging Pidgy's round sides she had tried to make the pony prance and toss her head as the Arabian did. But patient Pidgy, long used to thumping heels, plodded along evenly. She hadn't pranced since she was a filly and she had no intention of starting such nonsense now. Later, back

2

in the pasture, she grazed peacefully while Cindy
sat on the fence lost in misery over her.

"If only I had a horse," thought Cindy, "a beautiful spirited horse." Her dream was with her again,
her almost constant companion. In Cindy's daydreams wild and wonderful horses galloped and
leaped and pranced and tossed long silky manes
and tails. Cindy rode these shining creatures clinging to their smooth backs with her hands in their
flying manes . . . riding, riding, riding . . . while the
wind rushed by, whipping the color to her cheeks,
and the pounding of the horses' hoofs mingled

with the pounding of her heart. As she rode, there would be other horses, too, all around her; palominos, golden with the sunlight on their coats, their manes and tails like the white clouds; glistening, satiny blacks with fire-red nostrils, snorting; glossy bays and chestnuts rearing and plunging; a blur of pintos and dappled grays and duns. But never were there any ponies; only horses, horses, horses.

Everything was alive with them, pounding, snorting, neighing; a sea of flying manes and tails; the wonderful, heart stirring sound of horses. She could hear it; she could see it!

"Cindy, oh, Cindy!"

Suddenly the horses were gone. POP! They disappeared. Nothing remained. Nothing. Just Pidgy grazing. "Cindy, Cindy, where are you?"

Dazed, Cindy climbed off the fence. "I'm here, Mother, in the pasture," she called.

"Well, come and get washed up," called her mother. "Lunch is ready. Hurry up!"

"Just when I was going to ride that palomino, too," muttered Cindy. Pidgy walked up to her slowly. She reached her tiny head through the rails of the fence to nose the little girl's pockets for a morsel of sugar. Finding none, she stretched her neck to reach the untouched grass beyond the fence. Cindy fondled the pony's long forelock.

"You're all right, Pidge," she said. "But I still wish you were a horse."

"CINDY, will you PLEASE hurry!" came the call from the house. "Lunch is getting cold."

Pidgy lifted her head and watched Cindy run across the lawn and disappear. For a moment she stood with her ears pricked. Then the sweet grass called her back to her grazing. She would have laughed a little pony laugh if anyone had called her "poor Pidgy" then. She was very happy.

"Mother," said Cindy, thoughtfully toying with her soup, "when can I have a horse?" She asked it without emotion, already prepared for the usual negative answer. She had asked the same question many, many times.

"Cindy, dear, you know Daddy has told you the subject is not to be brought up again," said her mother wearily. "Why do you keep pestering when you know it is impossible to have another horse now?"

"But Pidgy's not a horse," protested Cindy. "She's a pony and besides . . . "

"Cindy!"

Her mother sighed. It was the same thing over and over again. Cindy was obsessed with the idea of having a beautiful and spirited horse of her own. Nothing ever occupied her mind but horses, always horses. Mrs. Sawyer looked across the table at her little dark-haired daughter. Cindy's blue eyes were misty again as they always were after she had been refused her horse. "Why, oh why doesn't she understand?" sighed Mrs. Sawyer to herself. "I'll just have to get Bob to talk to her again."

Cindy looked up at her mother's troubled face. She saw that further discussion of the subject would be hopeless. "I'm sorry, Mother," she said. "I guess I just can't help it. I keep hoping that maybe someday you'll say yes."

Tossing her long dusky braids over her shoulder, Cindy got up from the table. Stuffing her hands into the pockets of her faded blue jeans, she went toward the door.

"Cindy, you've hardly touched your lunch!" exclaimed Mrs. Sawyer. "Where are you going?"

"Oh, out to the barn. I haven't cleaned Pidgy's bridle yet and the bit's covered in green goo. She kept grabbin' at leaves when I rode her on Shaw's trail this morning," Cindy answered.

"Well, take this apple and here's one for Pidgy," said her mother quickly. "And you eat yours, don't give them both to Pidgy. And, Cindy," she added, "don't feel bad, honey. Remember you are lucky to have even Pidgy. Think of all the little girls who can only dream of having ponies."

"Dream, Mom, dream!" cried Cindy. "That's what I . . . oh, never mind . . . " She took the apples, and letting the screen door of the kitchen slam, she hurried down the steps and across the lawn.

"Such a silly girl!" murmured Mrs. Sawyer and she turned and began to clear away the lunch dishes.

Pidgy's Palace, as Mr. Sawyer laughingly called the little barn, stood in the corner of the back lawn. It was built of neat white boards in a kind of salt box style. There was a Dutch door entry and a little aisle separating a box stall and a small feed and tack room. Overhead was a loft which held a ton of baled hay. The stall had iron grill-work in front and the door latch was a slide bolt decorated with a tiny pony shoe. It had all been built especially for Pidgy three years earlier.

Glancing briefly at Pidgy who was still grazing at the far side of the pasture, Cindy went into the barn. She took the pony's bridle down from the rack. Walking to the shelf above the feed box, she picked up a sponge and dampened it in a pail of water. Then she set to work cleaning the thick green stain off the snaffle bit. It was hard work. She really had to rub to loosen the stubborn coating of color. As she worked Cindy's thoughts returned again to her horses. Which breed would she choose if the choice were hers now? Of all the beautiful horses in her dreams, which one would stand out? For which one would she give up all the others?

Cindy pondered. Her imagination called back all the shining steeds from their ranges in her mind. They came swiftly, galloping to her with eager whinnying and flying hoofs. "Which of us do you want, Cindy?" they seemed to ask as they milled around her. "Which of us do you choose?"

A lovely palomino reared up in the midst of the group. His glinting golden coat reminded Cindy of the bright dome of the state capitol which she had seen on a school trip not long ago. His mane and tail were like the splashing waters of West River Falls in the spring. He pawed the air for a moment, flaunting himself. Then he disappeared among the others. Cindy sighed. Surely there could be nothing more beautiful.

With a squeal another horse separated from the group. This was a piebald mare. She stood for a moment with her head held very high. Her eyes, white-ringed, burned into Cindy's own. A breeze stirred her mane, blowing her black forelock over her face. She squealed again, snorting at the others. They opened their ranks and she, too, disappeared.

"If I had her I would call her Night and Day," breathed Cindy.

Other horses presented themselves. They were on review; each trying to outdo the others in beauty and vitality. An American Saddlebred, a bay, appeared, with majestic, almost liquid action, seeming scarcely to touch the ground. He pranced momentarily, his silky mane and tail flowing about him. He arched his neck looking at Cindy with large lustrous eyes. Then he too wheeled and was gone.

Gradually all the horses disappeared, their color and brilliance fading like a summer sunset. Cindy sat on the overturned bucket in the feed room, with Pidgy's half-cleaned bridle in her lap. It was very quiet. There were no throbbing hoof beats, no piercing whinnies, no shining coats, no horses; just the gray light of the feed room and the green-stained bit on Pidgy's bridle.

Then suddenly there was a horse sound, a low nicker. Cindy jumped, startled. She turned quickly and there was Pidgy looking in the feed room door. There was a very mischievous pony expression on her face.

"Pidgy!" cried Cindy. "How in the world did you get out of the pasture?"

Pidgy had a talent for escaping from her pasture. Usually the pony stayed in the Sawyer's yard, although one time last month she had wandered away from home. Cindy was terribly upset and looked everywhere for Pidgy. The plucky pony was finally found at a nearby farm, peacefully grazing in a pasture with a handsome pony stallion. Cindy's father had 'Pidgy-proofed' the gate latch after that escape, but somehow Pidgy was still finding a way to get out.

Cindy's pony peered longingly toward the feed box and looked innocent. "No luck this time," her expression seemed to say. "It was so quiet in here I was sure there was no one around." She admonished herself for not waiting to be sure the barn was empty before attempting a raid on the feed box. Now Cindy had caught her in the act and would take greater precautions to keep her from getting out again. Pidgy's intelligent pony face was the picture of dejection as Cindy led her back to the pasture. The latch of the gate was unfastened. The pony had been working on it with her teeth.

"Now you get back in there and behave yourself, Pidge," said Cindy, slapping the pony smartly on the rump. "I can see Daddy is going to have to put an extra-strong pony-proof fastener on that gate for sure!"

GREENWOOD FARM

That night at the supper table, Cindy told her father about Pidgy's escape from the pasture. It was the third time this had happened in less than a month.

"She could get out of a bank vault!" laughed Mr. Sawyer. "She's a regular Houdini when it comes to getting out of things. Well, don't worry, honey, this time we'll get something to hold that gate that even little Miss Pidgy Houdini's brain will be no match for."

"Weren't you in the barn, Cindy?" asked her mother. "How could Pidgy have opened the gate without your hearing her? She must have made an awful racket fiddling around with that latch." Mrs. Sawyer looked questioningly at her small daughter.

"Well," began Cindy, "I was in the feed room and . . ."

"Cindy."

"Yes, Mother?"

"Did you clean Pidgy's bit?"

"Well, I . . . well, I'm almost finished with it," said Cindy.

"Cindy, were you daydreaming again?" probed Mrs. Sawyer.

"Ah . . ."

"Were you?"

"Yes, Mom, I guess I was just a little, but . . ."

"Cindy, how many times must we go over this with you? Your dreams of horses can only make you unhappy. You're getting to be a big girl now and you should realize, once and for all, that having horses as you dream them is simply impossible now, dear." Her mother spoke sympathetically but with finality, too.

"Come on, honey. Be happy with that little wizard Pidgy and forget all these wild stallions that hammer around in your head. You'd have a lot more than a gate latch to worry about if you had one of those creatures around the place." Mr. Sawyer laughed. He tossed his head and pawed the air, in his own imitation of a wild horse.

Cindy couldn't help smiling. "Oh, Daddy," she cried, jumping up from the table and throwing her arms around his neck, "you're so funny; my horses aren't like that at all!"

"Cindy, let's not hear any more about it, okay?" said Mr. Sawyer, looking seriously into his daughter's smiling face.

14

"No, Daddy, no more," whispered Cindy, suddenly sobered. "I won't say anything more about dream horses . . . only Pidgy."

But that night the phantoms galloped above Cindy's bed just the same. Pale horses: grays and duns and blue roans. They appeared luminous in the darkness. Their hoof beats were muted, almost soundless. Their shapes were shadowy and indistinct. When finally Cindy fell into the nothingness of sleep they carried her away with them to a gleaming place beyond the darkness.

U U U

The warmth of spring shimmered up from the ground in a steamy mist as Cindy and Pidgy trotted down the dirt road leading out of town. It was a Saturday in April and everything glistened with the joyous promise of approaching summer. Pidgy's little hoofs pattered briskly over the pebbly, rutted

road. The sound was cheerily rhythmic in the still-
ness of the morning. They were on their way to
Greenwood Farm and Pidgy knew it. The route was
familiar to her for they had made the trip many
times.

Cindy rode bareback, as she so often did. Her
blue jean clad legs scarcely gripped the pony's
sides, yet she was not insecure. She rode in a
relaxed, matter-of-fact way with the confidence of
one who is completely at home on a horse. People
often remarked, seeing her ride through town,
"That Cindy Sawyer goes along like she's a part of
that pony! Never saw a kid stick so well; riding
bareback, too!"

But Cindy didn't think of this at all. Riding to her
was just second nature. From the first moment she
was put on little Pidgy's back at her fifth birthday
party she had felt "at home." There had been no
fear, only a joyous delight that she was actually
riding her own pony! When the birthday party was
over and all the children had gone home, Cindy had
ridden her pony until it was almost dark. Her father
had led her around and around the lawn until the
fireflies had begun flickering in the shadows of the
big maple trees. And there had been a multitude of
stars pinpointing the night sky before she had
finally torn herself away. From then on she had
ridden almost every day, until soon she was able to
go by herself. Her complete lack of fear and a

friendly understanding for her mount had given Cindy her soft hands and firm seat.

Now as she and Pidgy clip-clopped along the narrow road, Cindy was thinking of the horses they were to see at Greenwood. Thoroughbreds were raised at the farm. There were usually colts and fillies racing around the paddocks and sometimes horses being schooled over the hunt course. It was always exciting to be at Greenwood in the morning when the young horses were being worked. Cindy urged Pidgy into a canter and they rollicked over the hill toward the farm.

Soon the stone walls lining the road gave way to neat post and rail fences and the acres of rolling pastures beyond were yellow-green with new spring grass. Cindy's heart thumped faster as she rode Pidgy through the gateway at Greenwood Farm. Here all her dreams became reality, for there

17

were horses everywhere. They frolicked in the high-fenced paddocks and peered at her from over the Dutch doors of their stalls. As she rode into the stable yard, a tall blond boy came from the building, leading a chestnut mare. He smiled broadly when he saw the little girl and her pony.

"Well, hi, Cindy!" he shouted, still beaming. "How's the girl and how's that wild 'n' beautiful steed of yours?"

Cindy flushed, but ignored the taunt. "I'm fine, Pete, and so's Pidgy. Thought we'd ride over and see how the horses are."

"Oh, then you didn't come to see me?" said Pete, looking hurt, but with a twinkle in his eyes. "Just the horses. Always the horses. Gosh, what's a fella to think when a girl comes riding five miles only to see the horses."

"Gee, Pete, I didn't mean just the horses!" cried Cindy anxiously.

"Never mind, Cindy, I know," Pete assured her. "I was only kidding. Here, put Pidgy in that empty stall and come on. I'm going to school this mare over the course. You're just in time to see some real action. Sis here can really jump!"

Cindy quickly put Pidgy in the stall, took off the pony's bridle, and then raced for the ring fence behind the stable, where she could get a good view of the course. Pete had swung into the chestnut's

19

saddle and was warming the mare up. Cindy watched, entranced. The horse's red coat glistened over the rippling muscles, catching the sunlight.

Pete finally turned her for the first fence, the mare's little ears pricked sharply forward and her eyes sparkled. Cindy caught her breath as the horse, increasing her speed, galloped toward the wide brush jump at the head of the course. Pete, leaning forward in the saddle, hands light but firm, steadied her as she neared the fence. With apparently no effort at all the horse soared over and raced for the next obstacle. Smoothly and brilliantly she judged each fence, taking them all in her ground-devouring stride. The course completed, the chestnut kept her hunting pace back to the ring where Cindy waited, still entranced.

"This one's a keeper!" said Pete as he eased the mare into a walk.

"Gosh, Pete, I'll say she is," breathed Cindy. "I've never seen her go so well. There won't be anything to beat her on the summer show circuit this year."

20

The boy smiled, patting the mare's glossy neck. He had trained her and was justly proud of his accomplishment. "Hank hates to admit it but Sis, here, can beat any of his show prospects this year," said Pete.

Hank Adams was Greenwood Farm's manager and trainer and there was always a friendly rivalry going on between the two. Pete being the owner's son made little difference in their friendship.

"Where's Hank this morning?" asked Cindy.

"Oh, he drove over to Woodbury to look at a horse someone's got for sale. Supposed to be a really 'hot' jumper," answered Pete.

"Gosh," exclaimed Cindy. "It must be wonderful to have all these terrific horses and always be ready to buy more, too. I'd be happy to have just one . . ."

"Spirited, beautiful horse," Pete laughed, finishing the sentence for her. "You'll have a horse some day, Cindy, don't worry. Meanwhile there's nothing wrong with Pidgy, you know. Come on, I have to walk Sis before she catches cold." Pete had never called the mare, Autumn Glow, anything but Sis since she was foaled. Now she was a four-year-old and the name still stuck.

They walked back to the stable together dis-
cussing Sis and her qualifications.

"Stick around, Cindy, I've got a few more horses
to work. Then I'll get Old Lew and ride home with
you," offered Pete.

For the rest of the morning, Cindy watched Pete
exercise Greenwood Farm's Thoroughbreds. She
hung on the rail fence and stored away all the
images of the beautiful animals her mind would
hold. It was material for endless dreams. She
watched carefully as Pete handled each horse. She
saw how the horses responded to his voice and his
hands. She saw the young ones prance and toss
their heads gaily and the mature ones take their
leads and their fences with the wisdom of age.
Cindy was in her element; inside her dreams . . .

When the last Thoroughbred was cooled out and back in its stall, Pete went to get Old Lew. He soon came out of the stable leading the old horse. Lew was a pinto, red and white. He had shaggy short legs and a hammer head. A striking contrast to his stablemates, he had once been a lead pony on the race track. He stood about fifteen hands and now in semi-retirement was rolling in fat. His mane and

tail were thick and coarse giving him the appearance, except for color, of a larger edition of Pidgy. But if looks were lacking, Old Lew had other redeeming features. He was good natured and quiet, his gaits were quite smooth, and he was absolutely trustworthy with other horses, the one qualification demanded of a lead pony.

"It seems funny to ride Old Lew after those 'hot' ones," exclaimed Pete as he and Cindy jogged down the road toward the village. "He's a good ole boy, though," he added, patting the pinto affectionately.

"You learned to ride on him, didn't you Pete?" asked Cindy.

"I sure did. And I can remember how I used to pester to ride something else. Oh, how I used to

beg! Hank would get so fed up sometimes he wouldn't even let me ride Lew. But then when the time came and I was ready, I had my chance on the 'hot' ones. And then there was Sis. So don't worry, Cindy, you've got lots of time for horses yet," Pete assured her.

"I guess so, only . . . " began Cindy.

"Come on," interrupted Pete, with a purpose. "Let's have a canter down to the next rise."

LET'S JUMP!

For the next few days, inspired by the thought of Pete's horse, Sis, and how she had done the hunt course at Greenwood Farm, Cindy was at work on a hunt course of her own. She had it all planned. If she couldn't have a horse which would jump like Sis, then she'd make a hunter out of Pidgy!

Out in the pasture Cindy constructed her fences. She made them of old fruit baskets and flower pots and all sorts of garden tools, such as Daddy's bamboo rake and his best oak-handled shovel. She took the low picket fence that protected Mom's petunia bed. She found an old laundry basket in the cellar and, covering it with evergreen branches, created a brush jump. Last year's plastic swimming pool made a most formidable water jump. And what could be better than the rose trellis for a gate?

After three afternoons of heaving and dragging and hammering and balancing, Cindy's hunt course was completed.

During all the construction activity, Pidgy had remained a disinterested bystander. She had cast a few questioning glances Cindy's way when the rose trellis, balanced on Cindy's head, had come around the corner of the barn. And she had been a little startled when Cindy appeared with the limp and crackly plastic swimming pool draped over her shoulders. But after the initial shock of seeing her pasture changed into a haven for assorted articles, Pidgy grazed undisturbed in the shadow of balanced flower pots and tipsy fruit baskets.

However, the next afternoon, when Cindy, home from school, came whistling into the pasture and called to her with new enthusiasm in her voice, Pidgy became suspicious. And when, after giving her a quick grooming, Cindy rode the pony back into the pasture, Pidgy became even more alarmed. She rolled her eyes and snorted at the baskets and pots as if she had never seen them before. The sight of the laundry basket brush jump filled her with

terror. Everything took on a new and fearful impor-
tance, for now they all somehow concerned HER!

Cindy walked the pony carefully around all the
obstacles, letting her sniff and snort as much as she
pleased. Pidgy took full advantage of the opportuni-
ty. She spooked and pranced and backed and
balked, unable to understand the meaning of all
this nonsense with garden tools.

Then, when the pony had given each "jump" a
disdainful snort, Cindy turned her toward the low-
est and least complicated of the obstacles. And suddenly it dawned on Pidgy that she was about to be
asked to jump the thing! Cindy's heels drummed
encouragement as they neared the fence: the row
of flower pots piled one on top of the other. But
Pidgy wasn't quite sure that something sinister
might not fly out from under one of the pots. Just
as she was supposed to jump she stopped . . . short!

Cindy, prepared for the worst, buried her hands in the pony's mane and hung on. Pidgy shook her head and snorted loudly. Then she began to back, still snorting her distaste for the flower pots. Before the pony had time to think, however, Cindy gave her a sound kick with both heels. Surprised at the suddenness of the blows, Pidgy sprang forward. Almost at once she was upon the flower pots. She had to jump this time or pile right into them. Pidgy jumped. She folded her forelegs neatly but one hind hoof struck a pot on the top layer. Clack! Crash!

Clatter! Like a row of toy soldiers the flower pots fell to the ground, scattered in all directions. Cindy gasped. Four of them lay broken in the grass.

But Pidgy was awake now and Cindy decided she'd better go on. She'd worry about the pots later. The next fence was crossed poles; or rather crossed garden rake and shovel. Each "pole" had one end resting on a large fruit basket and the other end on the ground. It was a simple arrangement and after the flower pots, there was nothing to fear. Pidgy cantered up to it. She pricked her little ears and popped over. Cindy patted her wildly.

31

"Good girl, Pidge!" she cried. "I knew you could do it!"

Full of confidence now, she sent the pony on for the next one: the laundry basket brush. Pidgy galloped up to it. Too fast! CRUNCH! Her hoofs came down right in the middle of the basket. Not ready this time, Cindy pitched over the pony's head and landed in a pile of evergreen boughs on the other side. Pidgy stood there with both forelegs in the basket looking hopelessly helpless. The picture the pony made standing in the brush fence sent Cindy into gales of laughter. She was still giggling as she lifted the pony's legs, one at a time, out of the basket.

"Lucky Mom doesn't use that basket any more, Pidge, or we'd be in trouble," said Cindy, mounting again. "Come on, let's try the rest of these fences."

Pidgy, however, had had just about enough of jumping. She had no intention of going over the rest of the course if she could help it, or even one more fence for that matter. As Cindy rode her into each obstacle she either ran through it, stopped and pushed it over with her shoulders, or wouldn't even go near it. Desperate, Cindy galloped the pony into the crossed poles again; the one she'd jumped so well in the beginning. But Pidgy "put on the brakes" at the last minute, and slammed into the bamboo rake on the fruit basket. Unable to pull back quickly enough, she stepped on the handle. There was a sharp crack! The rake fell down in two pieces.

Cindy was ready to admit defeat. The whole venture had been a failure. She looked at her hunt course. It was a shambles. Besides the broken flower pots and the laundry basket and the rake, there was a piece knocked off the rose trellis and Mom's petunia fence was minus three pickets. The plastic swimming pool would never hold water again, not with a hole the size of a pony hoof in the center of it!

Pidgy just wasn't meant to be a hunter.

I WANT A HORSE!

That evening before she went in to do her school work, Cindy walked out to the pasture again. She leaned against the fence and rested her chin on her hands. All around her everything was still except a few peepers down by the brook who were celebrating the arrival of spring. In the pasture the faint outline of the hunt course was still visible in the shadows. The picket fence and the rose trellis could be seen dimly in the soft light of a narrow new moon.

"All for nothing," sighed Cindy, looking at the dew covered course. "Pidgy will never be a jumper."

The warm darkness, the low-hanging new moon and the disappointment of the afternoon began to churn Cindy's imagination into motion. As she leaned on the top rail of the pasture fence looking at the dim shapes of the jumps, she thought she saw a movement in the willows by the brook. A soft mist was slowly drifting skyward from the peepers' home. It tangled in the budding branches of the willows before it faded finally from sight in the wide expanse of starry blue. From a set-

ting such as this could come any sort of whimsical being, but for Cindy Sawyer it had to be a horse.

He appeared from beyond the brook, as colorless and softly shadowed as the mist surrounding him. His dew-spangled hoofs sparkled briefly as he leaped the brook and stood on the bank beneath the willows, tasting the night wind. His long tail, like part of the mist, brushed the silver grass.

Suddenly from somewhere a frog croaked, a harsh, vulgar sound in the darkness. The phantom started. He sprang into the air, parting the clinging

mist. There was a throbbing, pulse-like beating in the air as the creature moved across the pasture, ghostly hoof beats in the shimmering grass. Cindy's hunt course lay ahead. All at once it loomed high. The pathetic flower pots and broken baskets were changed. In the gloom they became huge solid fences. The throbbing sound was deafening. The mist-phantom neared the first of the shadowy barriers. He rose as the mist rises from the brook, smoothly and gracefully, and then moved on. At each fence he leaped in a wide arc and galloped on to the next. Then, all at once, he was gone . . .

Cindy's hunt course was again fruit baskets and flower pots. The mist had lifted and disappeared. The peepers made the only sound. The slender new moon rested on the horizon hills almost out of sight.

"Make a wish, Cindy! Make a wish before it sets!"

But by the silvery pasture fence that April evening little Cindy Sawyer made not a wish but a vow: a vow that someday she would raise horses like the Phantom of the Mist.

U U U

After school the next day, Cindy put away all the pieces of her hunt course. She mended the rose trellis and replaced the pickets on Mom's fence and confessed and was quietly forgiven for the breakage of the flower pots and the bamboo rake. When everything was put away, Cindy bridled Pidgy and went for a ride.

She would have time just for a short jaunt, as the afternoon had flown by while she was cleaning away the hunt course and now it was only an hour till suppertime. Cindy decided to ride over to the Shaw's. Maybe their Arabian stallion would be out in the pasture. And maybe Alice would be there, too.

The trail to the Shaw's was the best in the country-side. It led off into the woods from the main road

north of town. Alice's father and brother were for-
ever cutting low-hanging branches and brush away
and picking up the endless quantities of rocks that
always seem to appear in woodland paths. They
kept the trail smooth and free of any kind of "stum-
ble material" from the town to their own driveway,
a distance of a mile and a half.

Cindy cantered along Shaw's trail whistling in
time to Pidgy's gait. The long shadows of late afternoon threw bluish stripes across the way, making it
seem as though a series of ditches were there to be
jumped. Cindy urged Pidgy into a faster canter. She
pretended they were hunting in Ireland and some of
the tree shadows were banks and some were ditches.
Thus occupied, it wasn't long before they reached the
place where the trail turned off into the Shaw's driveway. Cindy could see the barn and pasture beyond
the white colonial house. Suddenly there was a flash
of gray in the pasture. The Arabian was out!

Cindy slowed Pidgy to a trot, turning off the main drive toward the barn. Pidgy pricked her ears and nickered to the gray stallion in the field. With his plume of a tail like a long white banner, the horse trotted swiftly over to the fence. He seemed scarcely to touch the ground, so smooth and free was his action. Each hoof seemed to hesitate in mid-air a moment before it resigned itself to earth. As he reached the fence, he wheeled and struck out again across the pasture, this time at a gallop. He bucked and tossed his head playfully in sheer good spirits.

"The Sheik's showing off again."

Cindy, surprised at the voice, turned to see Alice Shaw standing behind her.

"Hi," said Cindy smiling at the dark-haired girl leaning casually against the barn door.

Alice Shaw was thirteen. Her slim, boyish figure, in tan jodhpurs, had the relaxed air of a person very sure of being able to command any situation, especially one pertaining to horses. In her own opinion, Alice was a top rider. She considered herself an authority on the subject 'horse' and was apt to lord it over the younger riders to show off her knowledge. But they all, including Cindy, looked up to her because with her own equitation horse or her father's hunter, Alice had won a room full of ribbons and trophies at horse shows. Therefore, since Cindy was just one of her many followers, Alice started right in coaching her.

"Why don't you ever ride that pony with a saddle? You'll ruin your form riding bareback all the time," she began. "How can you ever keep your elbows where they belong bouncing along like that?"

"I guess I just don't think about form, Alice, and a saddle is too much bother on Pidgy, anyway," answered Cindy.

"Well, you'd better think about it," said Alice, "or you'll never win a ribbon when you show." She was going to add, "If you ever show with that pluggy old pony," but thought better of it.

"Do you think they'll have any classes for ponies at the shows this summer?" Cindy asked hopefully.

"I don't know for sure. I was over at the club this afternoon and their show is scheduled for the end of June but they haven't decided about all the classes yet. Anyway, there probably won't be more than a couple; Lead Line and Pet Pony, that kind of stuff. Trouble is no one has ponies anymore. They couldn't fill the classes if they offered 'em. Not around here, anyway," said Alice, the voice of authority.

"Oh," said Cindy, crushed.

"Why don't you get your folks to buy you a horse? Then you could show all you wanted to," suggested Alice. Cindy ran her fingers through Pidgy's mane thoughtfully for a moment before she said, trying to be casual, "Oh, I guess I'll be getting a horse soon."

Alice looked at the younger girl closely. "Really?" she asked. "When?"

"Well, I don't know exactl8y, but sometime soon." Cindy lowered her eyes unable to meet Alice's piercing glance.

"What kind of a horse, Cindy?" asked Alice.

"I haven't made up my mind yet," Cindy said shakily. "I'm sort of looking around." She was frantic now to change the subject before Alice detect the lie in her voice. "Are you showing Sheik this summer?" she asked quickly.

Always glad to discuss her own doings with horses, Alice dropped the subject of Cindy's horse. "Probably my brother will take him in the breed classes and I might be riding him in the Parade Class at the club show," she said.

"He certainly is a beauty," sighed Cindy wistfully. "I'd sure like to ride him sometime."

"Oh, Don doesn't let anyone ride him but me," Alice stated importantly. "He's got a very sensitive mouth and Don says having a lot of people ride him isn't good for it. He goes beautifully for me, though. Want to see?"

"Gee, sure, Alice!" cried Cindy eagerly. "Shall I help saddle him?"

The Sheik allowed himself to be caught without too much trouble and submitted quietly to the process of saddling and bridling. Handled from a colt, he had not developed any of a stallion's bad habits, beyond an occasional display of good spirits. Before long Alice swung into the saddle and rode him back into the pasture. Cindy sat on the fence and watched.

The stallion moved across the field at a springy walk. His beautifully shaped head with its dished face was held high and he arched his neck gracefully with the play of Alice's fingers on the reins. They walked to the far side of the pasture. Then the horse broke into his smooth, gliding trot. It wasn't the same, nor as airy, as when he was loose but nonetheless it was lovely to see. He carried his tail high and proudly. It swept out behind him like a billowy flag.

Cindy was reminded of the Phantom of the Mist. The gray was almost like a dancer as Alice put him through his paces. Gallantly and gaily he obeyed her. "He's really enjoying himself," thought Cindy.

When the girl and the horse cantered back to the fence, Alice's face was shining. "He's terrific, isn't he?" she cried. "Don can really train a horse!" she added, applauding her brother.

Cindy helped unsaddle the stallion and then she untied Pidgy who all the while had grazed a circle around the post to which she had been fastened. Cindy jumped on the pony and waited for Alice to put the Sheik in his stall. Then they walked up the driveway together. It was getting late. Cindy said goodbye to Alice and hurried toward the trail.

"Let me know when you get your horse, Cindy," called the older girl. But Cindy's answer was lost on the wind as she cantered up the trail. Alice gazed a moment after the retreating pony and its rider. Then she shrugged thoughtfully and went back to the stable to give Sheik a good rubbing down.

GETTING READY TO SHOW

In her own room that night, Cindy sat at her desk doing her homework. The house was quiet. Mr. and Mrs. Sawyer were reading downstairs. There wasn't a sound except the hesitant scraping of Cindy's pencil as she struggled with her arithmetic problems. The lamp on the desk glowed down on her shining hair and also threw its light on a large photograph of Pidgy on the wall above. Below the picture, framed in a simple black molding, was an official looking document with the seal of a Shetland pony in one corner. It was Pidgy's pedigree and registration in the American Shetland Pony Club.

Cindy glanced up for a moment from a difficult problem in her textbook. Her eyes rested on the photograph of Pidgy and then fell to the pedigree . . . Silver Eagle's Pigeon 2356 . . . Sire: Silver Eagle II, Dam: Little Peanut. The document went on to name her grandsire and granddam back three generations.

"Oh, Pidgy's well-bred all right—as pure bred as even Sheik or Sis—but," thought Cindy, "it doesn't make her more beautiful or spirited or anything. She's still just a pony; a plain, fuzzy pony for all the high-sounding names on her pedigree."

Cindy looked again at the photograph. It showed Pidgy as summery slick as she ever would be, standing in the pasture. Her father had snapped the picture just as the pony had lifted her head a moment from her grazing. There were a few spears of grass sticking from the corners of her mouth and she appeared to be chewing vigorously. Cindy smiled as she always did when she looked at the picture. Poor funny little Pidge—always the clown—even in the show ring; almost winking at the spectators on the rail, never paying any attention to Cindy's frantic urgings, just clowning all the time. Pidgy not only wasn't a hunter, she wasn't a show pony either.

Suddenly Cindy thought about her conversation with Alice Shaw. Why had she ever told the older

girl that she was going to get a horse? Now Alice would never stop asking her about it. Oh, if only it were true; a horse like The Phantom, hers at last. She looked at Pidgy's picture again. This time she didn't smile, for she was not really looking at the picture at all but through it. In her imagination she had escaped beyond the limited boundaries of the frame and had ridden her phantom away into the endless mists.

Later, coming into Cindy's room to say good-night, Mrs. Sawyer found her little girl asleep at her desk. Her hand rested on the open math book; her pencil had fallen to the floor. The soft lamplight gently shaded the smile on her face. Cindy was far away again in her golden dream.

Mrs. Sawyer sighed softly. "Horses . . ." she said.

U U U

Spring days lengthened and warmed into early summer. The promises of plump buds and bird songs were fulfilled at last. The earth seemed to swell everywhere with a contagious joy. All things seemed to smile. Trees in their shiny new leaves whispered and giggled like school-girls sharing a secret. The high, glowing sun soaked the country-side with life-giving warmth. And the rainy days only made the sunny ones seem brighter.

But on this particular sparkling day in early June, Cindy Sawyer rode home from Alice Shaw's farm sunk in gloom that was very much out of step with the rest of the smiling world. She kept her pony at a walk even when long smooth stretches of the trail were just shouting an invitation for a brisk canter. Even Pidgy champed a little to be off at a faster gait. This was like a funeral march! But Cindy, head bent in misery, wasn't thinking about cantering or the radiance of the day. She wasn't even thinking about Pidgy.

No, Cindy was thinking about the horse show soon to be held at the nearby country club. She was thinking about Alice Shaw and her equitation horse, Red Chief, and Alice's brother Don and his Arabian, and Mary Pat Winters' Thoroughbred hunter, and Jane Randall's Morgan, and of Pete Greene and his beautiful Sis, and of all the others who had HORSES. She thought of what the horse show would be for them: of all the classes there were for horses. Then she thought of Pidgy. There would be only two for Pidgy. Her thoughts suddenly slipped, as they were bound to, back to the conversation with Alice that morning. It had been partially responsible for the cloud of gloom which had settled so densely over Cindy's youthful shoulders.

She finally had to admit to Alice that she wasn't really getting a horse after all. It had been a very painful task. And the worst of it had been the fact that Alice said she had known it all along.

"Do you know how I guessed it, Cindy?" Alice had asked. "I knew because if you actually were about to get a horse of your own, you'd have come high-tailin' it over here to tell me as fast as that pony of yours could travel. You were just too casual about it to be convincing. I know you, Cindy, you can't hold anything you feel inside; it just busts right out of you. That's how I guessed you were fibbing. But cheer up, they have decided to have the small division of Children's Hacks and Pet Ponies, too, at the show this year. So you can still show, anyway."

After telling Cindy that she had seen through her fib, Alice had proceeded to relate in glowing terms how well Red Chief was going and how she had such a good chance of winning the blue in the Advanced Horsemanship Class; and also that she was definitely going to ride Sheik in the Parade Class, too. Alice's enthusiasm had soon completely blotted out all the sunshine for Cindy.

Now she and Pidgy neared home and the bright cheerfulness of the day had failed to dispel her gloom. She rode into Pidgy's pasture, took off the pony's bridle and went slowly into the house. Pidgy rolled luxuriously for a moment and had a cool drink from the brook. Then she began to graze peacefully. It had been an easy day for the pony.

"Bob, we've got to do something about Cindy," exclaimed Mrs. Sawyer one evening a few weeks later.

"Why, what's the matter with her?" asked her husband, scarcely looking up from his paper.

"Do you mean you haven't noticed anything? Anything at all?" said Mrs. Sawyer.

"Well, no . . . no, I can't say I have."

"Oh, Bob, the child's miserable."

"She is?" Mr. Sawyer put down his paper finally and listened fully to what his wife was saying.

"She's still dreaming about horses—one horse really—a horse of her own," explained Mrs. Sawyer.

"What's wrong with Pidgy? She used to adore that little devil. What's she want a horse for when she's got Pidgy to ride?" asked Mr. Sawyer.

"A pony's apparently not the same, Bob. She listens to Alice Shaw tell her about horses and then there are the others at the club and she, well, she feels left out. The girls are all riding in the club show next week, all kinds of classes, and Pidgy's only got two. And well, you know how Pidgy always clowns

around all the time. I tell you Cindy's miserable." Mrs. Sawyer wrung her hands in a gesture of desperation.

"Janet, I had no idea Cindy felt that way. I always thought her grumbling about horses all the time was just the usual kid's daydreams. Apparently it's more than that," said Mr. Sawyer, quite disturbed.

"She desperately wants a horse, Bob, that's all she thinks about."

"But we can't get her one now. We've tried to explain it to her. She should realize it by now; after all she's old enough."

"She knows she can't have one but it doesn't stop her daydreaming and wishing all the same. If only there were something we could do to get her mind off these wild and beautiful creatures in her dreams and back with her Pidgy again."

∪ ∪ ∪

A few days later while shopping in the village, Mrs. Sawyer met Pete Greene.

"Hello, Pete, how are you?" she said. "I haven't seen much of you lately. How is everything at Greenwood?"

Pete's blue eyes sparkled. "I'm fine, Mrs. Sawyer, and we are all really busy at the farm these days with the show season coming up," answered Pete smiling. "How's my girl, Cindy? Still dreaming of a 'wild 'n' beautiful' horse of her own?"

"I'm afraid she is, Pete," answered Mrs. Sawyer.
"Though it isn't anything that she says—Bob made
her promise not to say any more about it—but her
dreams are still there as vivid as ever. Really, Pete,
I don't know what we are going to do with her. Even
Pidgy doesn't make her happy any more."

"Pidgy's a good pony; as trustworthy as they
come. Cindy's had a lot of good times with her. It's
too bad she doesn't realize it," said Pete, shaking his
head.

"It's those dreams of hers and also the fact that girls like Alice Shaw and Mary Pat Winters have horses and do so much talking about showing and winning ribbons all the time," sighed Mrs. Sawyer.

"Alice's Red Chief isn't such a wonderful horse," scoffed Pete. "He's just a machine; trained to the hilt by a professional. That's why he wins so much. He's not so much on conformation and I just bet that Alice hasn't had nearly as much fun with him—aside from winning at the shows—as Cindy has had with little Pidgy. Gosh, but it's too bad we can't make Cindy realize that and get her interested in the pony again."

"That's just what Bob and I were saying. But how, Pete? Any ideas?" asked Mrs. Sawyer.

"Well," thought Pete, "can't think of anything right now. But I'll let you know if I get any ideas."

"Thanks, Pete," said Mrs. Sawyer. "I appreciate any suggestions."

THE COUNTRY CLUB
HORSE SHOW

Suddenly it seemed it was late in June and the show season had begun. The first show and the only one for Cindy and Pidgy was at the Country Club. It was an annual affair which attracted local riders and spectators to the modest little ring beside the golf course. The Country Club Horse Show was always a lively and friendly affair with enough classes and competition to keep the horse owners happy and the spectators interested.

Without too much enthusiasm, Cindy groomed her pony for the show. Pidgy, now shed of her woolly winter coat was a slick sort of milk-chocolaty brown. She seemed to enjoy the vigorous brushing and mane and tail combing she was being given even though it was brief. Mostly, though, she just enjoyed the attention. Cindy had not acted very happy or very interested in any kind of adventures lately. Pidgy remembered when they had gone on exciting jaunts almost every day. And now all the zest had disappeared from their rides. Now they only walked; either to the Shaw's or out to Greenwood to watch the horses being schooled. And Cindy was always so quiet, hardly ever speaking or laughing or whistling any more. Maybe she's

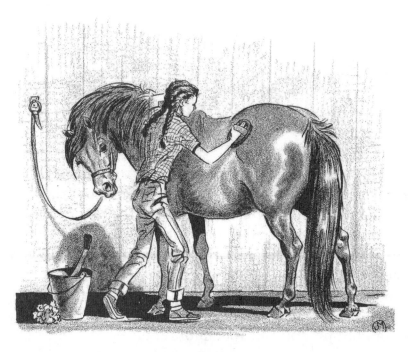

snapping out of it now, thought the pony. Anyway, the brushing feels good!

An hour later Cindy rode a slick and shining Pidgy, saddled for a change, up the trail to the country club. That her hopes were dim could be seen by looking at her face. Her eyes had the mournful far away look which was almost her sole expression of late. She wore neat tan jodhpurs and a short sleeved yellow shirt. Her hair, braided carefully, was tied with yellow ribbons. The browband of Pidgy's bridle she had also decorated, at her mother's suggestion, with yellow ribbon left over from her braids. If Cindy had only worn a smile, the effect would have been perfect.

Horse show hustle and bustle was at its height when Cindy and Pidgy rode into the country club. People called to her merrily; some on horseback, some in cars, some walking. They were all surprised at her serious expression. It just wasn't like Cindy Sawyer to be that glum. Wonder what's happened? Pony looks fine. Strange.

Pete Greene, riding Sis, made his way through the light-hearted, milling crowd. Suddenly he saw Cindy and her pony.

"Hi!" he called standing in his stirrups. "CINDY!" He put Sis into a jog and hurried up to them.

"Where've you been? I've been looking all over for you."

"Hello, Pete," said Cindy forcing a smile. "I...I guess I'm a little late."

"Not very; they are just running off the Model Classes now. Your class is right after mine, the Green Hunters. You can sit on Pidge and watch me win it!" said Pete jokingly. "How's that?"

Cindy brightened a little. "I bet you will win, Pete. Sis is wonderful!"

They rode through the throng of enthusiasts to the Greenwood Farm trailer. There Hank was holding a sleek bay gelding. A blue ribbon hung from the horse's bridle.

"Howdy, Cindy. Pony looks good, kid," said Hank all in one breath. His face crinkled into a smile. "You gonna take a few of these home with you today?" he asked flipping the ribbon on the bay's bridle.

"I don't know, Hank," answered Cindy, her spirits a bit brighter.

"Sure you will. Pidgy's the best pony hereabouts or my name's not Hank Adams."

It was then that the public address system called over the crowd for a Horsemanship Class.

"Alice is in this one," said Pete. "Let's ride over and see how she makes out. See you later, Hank."

The tall, good-looking blond boy on the chestnut Thoroughbred and the little pigtailed girl on the

small fat pony made an appealing picture as they jogged down to the show ring. Hank Adams watched them a moment, grinning, and then he began to walk the bay gelding toward the water trough under the trees.

Alice and Red Chief were already trotting briskly around the ring when Cindy and Pete rode up.

"Pretty good grandstand seats, eh, Cindy?" said Pete, arranging a braid on Sis' neck. "Well, now let's see if Miss Alice-Smarty-pants is as good as she thinks she is."

Out in the ring the last entry had come through the gate and the class was complete. There were twelve riders altogether; each grim and determined to take home the silver trophy. Their faces wore stony expressions as they concentrated on their form. Each was faultlessly dressed in correct show attire and every horse was groomed to within an inch of its life. The red-coated ringmaster called the class down to a walk while the judges marked numbers on their cards. The battle—dignified but nonetheless a battle—had begun.

"Alice will have to really do her stuff to win in this company. The competition is terrific!" exclaimed

Pete. "Look at the boy on that little bay with the white socks, he can't be more than fourteen but he's spinning around that ring like a veteran."

But Cindy's interest was not as much in the riders as in the horses. She somehow preferred to watch the sunlight playing on glossy coats and the graceful way their tails blew when they cantered. She had watched Alice awhile and had soon grown tired of the cold perfection of her riding. To Cindy, Alice seemed almost stiff in her faultlessness. She never made a mistake. At each gait her aids were imperceptible and Red Chief seemed almost to read her mind, so fluently did he move from one gait to

another. It was soon plain to see that no other horse in the ring was quite so well trained. There seemed to be a flaw in each of them; one tossed his head constantly, clanking his bits; another broke his canter at a crucial moment; another didn't like his left lead. But Red Chief, the highly trained, the obedient, ears up and eyes bright, moved through the judges' commands as smooth as glass. Alice's set face wore a rather smug expression after having completed a figure eight to perfection. She rode back into the line to watch the others take their turns. A few went quite well; others, however, got results from their horses only with much pounding of heels.

"Guess Alice's got this one sewn up," observed Pete resignedly. "And I bet you won't be able to touch her with a ten foot pole when she comes out. The boy on the bay will get second, though, and he's not too far behind her at that."

As Pete had predicted Alice won the class without dissent from anyone. When her number was called she rode Red Chief to the center of the ring to accept the big silver trophy. She smiled at the judges and the grandstand but, Cindy noticed, failed to give Red Chief the pat on the neck which was certainly due him. Photographers took pictures and applause rippled through the spectators. When the little boy on the bay was given second, his face broke into a toothy grin and, dropping his reins, he thumped his horse wildly on the neck with both hands. His joy

was boundless. The clapping and cheering increased in volume as the red ribbon was pinned on the bay's bridle. It was clear that although Alice Shaw's performance was "blue ribbon material" the sympathy of the crowd had been with the rider of the little bay.

As Alice rode out of the ring she handed the trophy matter-of-factly to her brother, Don, waiting at the gate. Cindy watched and was amazed to see her lack of enthusiasm. A few words passed between the girl and her brother and then Alice rode over to Pete and Cindy.

"Not much competition in that class," she said rather haughtily as she rode up. She evidently hadn't paid much attention to the boy on the bay. If the truth were known, she had not won the class by much of a margin. Indeed he might have placed first had his little horse not gotten off on the wrong lead once when the judge was watching him.

Alice Shaw was typical of many young riders showing in the summer circuit. She was without question a good rider. Yet, although she never mistreated a horse, she lacked the sympathy for her mount which marks the true horsewoman. She learned all she could about horses and did everything correctly down to the last detail but it was for her own glorification that she did it; only so people would say, "Alice Shaw knows all about horses and showing," and "Alice Shaw has a roomful of trophies," and, "Alice Shaw has her picture in the papers all the time."

All at once the show announcer's call for horses in the Green Hunter Class interrupted Alice's monologue on how she had won the Horsemanship Trophy.

"That's us, Sis!" said Pete, glad of an excuse to get away from the self-centered girl. "See you, Alice." And to the little girl on the pony he added, "You'll get a better view of the course on that rise, Cindy." Then he swung Sis's head toward the group of horses and riders at the In Gate of the ring.

"Pete Greene thinks he's hot stuff, doesn't he?" said Alice irritably. He hadn't fallen for her line and she knew it.

"He is!" answered Cindy brightly and, nudging Pidgy, rode off.

Alice looked after the younger girl trotting toward the hill. She had a feeling she was losing an admirer.

The outside course consisted of eight varied fences as close as possible to the type to be found when hunting. Entries were required to start over a brush fence out of the ring and finish back over a white gate into the ring.

The hunters quietly waited their turn. Although they were young – three, four, and five year olds – they, for the most part, stood without fidgeting. Some watched intently with high heads and pricked ears as the other horses negotiated the course. One pawed the ground, anxious to be next. When it came time for Sis to go, Pete pulled down his black velvet hunt cap, picked up the laced reins of the mare's bridle and jogged into the ring. The announcer called his number. Leaning forward, Pete put the mare into a slow canter, made a little circle and turned her for the brush fence. The little golden braids flopped on the horse's neck as she

moved toward the jump. She flicked her tail playfully before, right in her stride, she soared over the
brush. They were on their way!

From the hill Cindy watched breathlessly, her
fingers crossed under Pidgy's heavy mane. The
beautiful chestnut mare flew over each fence as
consistently and brilliantly as she did at home. Pete
sent her into one after another with careful timing.

"She's going to win! She's going to win!" whispered Cindy fervently into Pidgy's ear. She could
hardly contain her excitement as horse and rider
galloped down a slope toward the stone wall. Sis's
gait changed ever so slightly as she neared the solid
looking obstacle. Pete steadied her. Cindy could not
hear him but she knew he was speaking to the
mare in soothing tones. The wall loomed high. With
a powerful drive of her glossy hindquarters Sis

sprang from the ground. In mid-air she seemed to falter. Cindy gasped, squeezing her fingers into Pidgy's mane. There were two dull thuds as the

chestnut mare's hind hoofs struck the log on the top of the wall. As she landed she seemed almost to fall. Cindy heard a groan swelling from the crowd. But then the mare regained her balance and was soon back in her stride. The tension lessened. What happened, what happened? Cindy's brain clamored the question as Sis galloped for the last fence. Pete's hand was on her sweating neck as Sis came to the white gate. The boy gave the straining horse her head and she sailed over like a bird. Loud applause burst from the spectators as horse and rider galloped the length of the ring. Cindy stood in her stirrups and cheered wildly. A minute later Pete jogged up to her.

"What happened, Pete, what made Sis almost fall?" cried the child.

"Ground's all chewed up down by that wall. Sis must have stepped on a stone. Anyway, she sort of lost her balance. I could feel it when she jumped. I think the stone rolled as she left the ground, throwing her off. The landing side is almost as bad, too. Oh, well, those things happen. Sis took all the other fences perfectly." Pete patted the mare's wet neck. He was disappointed but he did not blame her.

When the last hunter had completed the course all the riders were called back to the ring. Each one trotted his horse before the judges for soundness. Then the ringmaster was handed the cards which he brought to the announcer.

"We have the results of the Green Hunter Class," blared the public address system. "First, Number 35, Blue Angel; Second, Number 8, Country Lad; Third,—" Cindy held her breath. "Number 15, Knight Errant; Fourth, Number 5, Autumn Glow."

It was all over. Pete rode out with the white ribbon fluttering from Sis's bridle.

"Well, Cindy, you're next. Get in there and win a blue for Sis 'n' me." Pete smiled through his disappointment. "I'll have an eye on you!"

CINDY AND PIDGY
ENTER THE RING

J ust before she rode into the ring, Cindy saw her mother and father up in the grandstand. Mr. Sawyer held up crossed fingers as Pidgy jogged through the gate. As soon as she felt the hundreds of eyes upon her, Cindy stiffened a little. She heard the announcer call the rest of the Children's Hacks to the class.

"Children's Hacks, Small Division. Bring them up, please."

There were a few other Shetlands in the class but almost at once Cindy knew she and Pidgy were only in there for the ride. Sleek, almost miniature Thoroughbreds with braided manes and tails, and slim-legged Welsh ponies trotted perfectly around the green oval of the ring. Pidgy trotted too—her cute, bouncy, little-pony trot—and Cindy posted evenly. A few people smiled as they went by. Pidgy was so fat that her sides shook up and down when she moved. Her long bushy tail brushed the ground behind her and she peered through her heavy forelock with bright and sparkly eyes. She was thoroughly enjoying herself. But the best was yet to come!

"Walk, please!" came the command from the ringmaster.

Six ponies walked. But one little girl on a spotted Shetland trotted briskly the length of the ring before she succeeded in bringing the pony down to a jiggly walk. Her pained expression sent ripples of mirth running through the grandstand. Cindy's mouth, however, was a firm straight line. She dare not laugh in case the same happen to her.

When all the entries in the class were finally walking in a civilized manner, the command came to trot. Cindy touched Pidgy's round sides with her heels. Nothing happened. The pony continued to walk. Her eyes were fixed on the rump of the pony ahead of her. Cindy heeled her again. Pidgy swished her long tail sassily and broke into a bouncy trot. Thus they went around the ring; Pidgy still swishing her tail up and down and eyeing the spectators along the rail. She snorted at them and tossed her

head as she bounced along. The yellow ribbons on
Cindy's braids bobbed up and down as they moved
around the ring.

All the show ponies slowed to a walk at the next
command and miraculously Pidgy did the same.
The spotted Shetland, however, had other ideas.
He decided to take a short cut. Before his youthful
rider could stop him, he ducked his head and ran
across the ring at a choppy canter. In the nick of
time the frightened child on his back put all her
strength on the right rein and turned him before
he ran down one of the judges. Cindy flinched.

Although she knew Pidgy was hardly that sort of pony it didn't help ponies in general to have that sort of thing going on.

The judge who had "been in the line of fire" mopped his brow and told the ringmaster to have them canter. He probably would be glad when the class was over and at this point felt he had slim chance of getting out alive.

At the canter Pidgy behaved herself—at least for awhile. She took the correct lead and rollicked around gaily as if she were on Shaw's trail. The judges were looking at her, too, but Cindy kept her mind on her work and only noticed them out of the corner of her eye. Outside the ring, Pete thought, you're doing fine, Cindy.

As Pidgy came around by the grandstand again a little boy with a large red lollypop reached through the rail directly in front of the cantering pony.

"Pony want thum?" he lisped, holding out the candy.

Too late Cindy realized what would happen. And it did! Pidgy stopped short. Only by luck and good balance did Cindy remain in the saddle. The pony made an eager grab for the red lollypop, badly frightening the little boy. He dropped the candy into the dirt, and screamed as though all the demons of darkness were after him. The grand-

stand was in an uproar. Someone shouted, "That pony bit that little boy! Call a doctor! Call the S.P.C.A.! Call an ambulance!"

It had all happened so suddenly that Cindy was stunned beyond thought. She backed Pidgy away from the rail and, flushing violently, waited to see what developed. The ringmaster was dashing around calling the riders to walk, which of course they'd already done, and the announcer was frantically telling everyone to keep calm and getting more excited himself at every word. The judges looked exactly like boiled lobsters!

Finally the screaming little boy stopped screaming. "I want my 'ollypop, I want my 'ollypop," he whimpered.

"Did the bad pony bite you, sonny?" someone asked.

"No, but I want my 'ollypop," he wailed.

When the news that Pidgy hadn't bitten the child after all circulated through the grandstand, everyone settled down. There was a hum of voices and the announcer's rose above it all, still too loud and too high-pitched, but the crisis had passed. The judges mopped their brows and nodded to the ringmaster to carry on with the class. They probably wondered if they really would live through the day!

After order had been restored, the class continued as before. Soon the ringmaster, his voice calm and authoritative again, directed the riders to line up. Cindy had not fully recovered from the lollypop incident even though Pidgy had behaved herself quite well afterwards. Cindy would be very glad when the class was over. She could still see people pointing at her and Pidgy and it made her very self-conscious. Once she had glanced up at her father. He had motioned to her to keep her chin up.

Suddenly the announcer cleared his throat as the ringmaster handed him the judges' cards. "We have the results of—Harumph—the Children's Hack Class, Small Division (this with emphasis): First, Number 14, Jill's Boy; Second, Number 23,

Little Lark; Third, Number 42, Snowman; Fourth, Number 53, Bright Star."

The ribbons were all awarded and the gate swung open. The ponies and riders began to file out. As Cindy turned Pidgy to leave, one of the judges walked up to her.

"That was an unfortunate mishap, young lady, we all liked your pony. Better luck next time."

Cindy managed a smile and a "thank you" and then she rode out of the ring. Pete and Mr. Sawyer met her at the gate. "Well," said her father. "You and Pidgy put on quite a show! They'll be talking about it around here for days!"

Cindy swallowed hard. "It wasn't Pidgy's fault. It just wasn't. That little boy stuck his lollypop right out under her nose. She had to stop!"

Pete winked at Mr. Sawyer. "Of course she did, Cindy. Come on, I'll buy you a soda."

"Go ahead, honey, I'll hold Pidgy," offered her father. As Cindy and Pete headed for the refreshment tent, Mr. Sawyer led Pidgy toward the water trough. "Let's go and get you a drink, too, little girl. You've had quite a time," he said to the pony.

There were no more incidents and by the middle of the afternoon the judges seemed actually to be enjoying themselves. Each class ran off in good time and smoothly. The horses shown were of fine type and in excellent condition.

Pet Ponies, Cindy's other class came just before the Championship Classes. Most of the afternoon she had sat in the grandstand with her mother and father watching the show. She had seen Pete and Sis win the Lightweight Hunter Class and also the Hunter Hacks. She watched Alice and Red Chief taste defeat to Mary Pat Winters' Thoroughbred, in the Large Division of Children's Hacks. The Parade Class, however, had put Alice on top again. She had won without any question with the Sheik. During the class, Cindy had not been able to hide her admiration for the gray stallion in the shining silver-mounted equipment. The other horses were common dobbins compared to the light-footed, graceful Arabian with his flowing mane and tail.

When it came time for her class, Cindy left her parents in the grandstand and hurried to Greenwood Farm's trailer where Pidgy was tied. The little mare nickered softly when she saw her young mistress approaching.

As she slipped the bridle over the pony's ears, Cindy felt anxiety rising within her once more. Would something unforeseen happen in her class this time too? Pete had assured her that it had been tough luck, like Sis stumbling on the stone in the Green Hunter Class, and not to let it bother her. With a firmly set jaw, Cindy mounted her pony and went down to the ring. Other children were waiting in groups for the announcer to call them for the Pet Pony Class. Most of them rode Shetlands, too. The little girl with the spotted pony, who had nearly run

down the judge in the Children's Hack Class, was there looking grim and determined not to let it happen again. And there were also five small, mischievous looking little ponies waiting their turn to be in the limelight.

Finally the announcer called them in. There were the usual "Ohs" and "Ahs" and "aren't they cute" from the spectators and a few murmurings about the earlier class. Cindy and Pidgy were pointed out again but she forced herself to ignore the voices mentioning her name. As they walked around the ring she searched the grounds for sight of Pete. She saw him, mounted on Sis, talking to another rider on a hunter. She hoped he would watch her class.

The long day was nearing its close as the children and their ponies walked, trotted and cantered around the ring. The summer sun's rays had begun to slant long shadows on the scene. A few more classes and the Country Club Horse Show would be over for another year. There was a definite lessening of enthusiasm in the exhibitors—except those riders up for championships—and already some of the spectators were moving toward their cars.

But in the ring the youngest riders were doing their best to go home with a ribbon. And Cindy was doing best of all! At each command the little chocolate brown mare did as she was asked; right lead, left lead, walk, trot, turn. She was no longer Pidgy the clown. Cindy's face was shining as the ringmaster told them to line up. She looked quickly beyond the ring fence for Pete. He winked at her from Sis's back. Pidgy's had a change of heart and it's come at a good time, he mused to himself. She should take this class.

And that's exactly what happened! When the announcer called her number, Cindy was dumbfounded with joy. "Pidgy, Pidgy!" she cried. "Oh, Pidgy, we won, we won!" And she patted the pony's neck wildly. Up in the stands Mr. and Mrs. Sawyer looked at each other and smiled very satisfied smiles. Pete Greene smiled, too, as he watched his happy little friend receive the silver trophy and the blue ribbon. When the other ribbons had been awarded, one of the judges walked up to Cindy and said, "Well, young lady, feel a little better now?"

"Oh, yes," breathed Cindy clutching the trophy tightly in her moist hands.

"That's a very nice pony," continued the judge. "Bet you have a lot of fun with her, don't you?"

"Oh, yes, I do," replied Cindy. Then her shining face clouded a little. "But sometimes I wish very hard that I had a horse."

The judge laughed and patted Pidgy on the rump. "Time enough for that, young lady, time enough for that!" He had heard the same sort of thing from many children, including his own! "You just take good care of that pony," he urged her.

Cindy assured him that she would and smiling her most engaging smile she rode from the ring. They were all there to greet her as she came

through the gate: Mother and Daddy and Pete and Hank and even Alice.

"Well, I should say Pidgy surprised us all!" exclaimed Mr. Sawyer. "Pidgy the EX-clown!"

Everyone laughed.

"I guess she made up for this morning, all right," admitted Alice soberly.

"Didn't I tell you you'd bring home a blue with that pony, Cindy?" Hank asked, grinning from ear to ear.

"Nice going, honey," said Pete simply. But Cindy knew he was the most pleased of all.

The sun was hanging low and red on the edge of the hills when Cindy surrendered her trophy to her parents and turned Pidgy toward the village. She could have sent Pidgy home in Greenwood Farm's trailer but somehow she felt she wanted to ride. Since it was such a short way she had succeeded in talking her family into letting her do this. The blue ribbon still fluttered from the pony's bridle. Cindy had refused to part with it even for a moment.

As she rode along the shadowy trail letting Pidgy walk at her own speed, Cindy's "dream horses" whinnied to her from a farther range. And standing ahead of them all in the summer twilight was a chocolaty-brown pony with a blue ribbon hanging in its mane.

Let's Go Swimming!

After the Country Club Horse Show was a thing of the past, summer days seemed to fly by faster than ever. Each glistening misty morning or sultry afternoon found Cindy and Pidgy together. The pony's blue ribbon had saved the summer for Cindy. Now although her "dream horses" still moved through her imagination, as Mr. Sawyer said, "They didn't bother Cindy at all!" Cindy still wanted a horse but she resigned herself to waiting. Sometimes watching Sis or Sheik it became difficult for her to keep from wishing fervently once more but she had only to think of Pidgy's ribbon and maybe others she would win and the clamoring steeds became quiet again.

Mr. Sawyer noticed the change in his daughter and remarked to his wife, "I think our Cindy is growing up!"

U U U

One hot afternoon in late August, Pidgy's cease-less grazing was interrupted by her young mistress' hurried footsteps approaching the pasture.

"Come on, Pidge," she cried. "We're going swimming!" She fumbled with the heavy "pony proof" gate fastener, which Mr. Sawyer had put on after one of many escapes by the sly pony.

Pidgy walked up to Cindy, nickering softly. Cindy produced the inevitable piece of carrot and quickly led the pony out of the pasture into the little barn. After a hasty grooming, Pidgy was swiftly bridled. Then, leaping on the mare's round back, Cindy rode her up the driveway at a fast trot. The August sun boiled down with a vengeance as pony and rider turned into an overgrown trail on the outskirts of the village. Trees heavy with summer leaves shaded the path from the merciless, scorching sun and it seemed as though there must be millions of invisible birds chirping and chattering in the thick foliage.

Cindy whistled merrily. She was anxiously anticipating the cool swim in Randall's Pond. At last her mother had weakened and said that she could go, but only because Pete was going to be there to watch her. Pete had called Mrs. Sawyer (at Cindy's pleading) and said he would ride Old Lew over to the pond and keep an eye on the energetic Cindy.

Now, extra warm because of her swim suit under her jeans, Cindy thumped her pony's sides and encouraged her into a slow canter.

Randall's Pond was a little blue gem, bordered by tall pines on one side and a wide expanse of meadow on the other. A little gurgling brook fed sparkly clear water into it all summer long even after other ponds had been reduced to green-scrummed, stagnant pools in the heat. A rough raft with a creaky diving board had been made by some of the older boys of the town, and now as Cindy neared the place the cries and splashes and shrieks of delight assured her that someone was making good use of the pond's attractions. As soon as she rode out of the woods Cindy saw Pete. He was sitting cross-legged on Old Lew talking to some of the children at the edge of the water.

"Hi, Pete!" she called loudly. "Have you been here long?"

"No, Cindy, just got here," said Pete. "Want me to hold 'Wild 'n' Beautiful' for you while you swim?" Pete couldn't resist the little dig about Cindy's Dream Horse when he knew she would take it good-naturedly.

"Oh, Pete," Cindy feigned exasperation at the old jest. "Yes, would you hold Pidgy for me, please?" She put emphasis on the name. Then she struggled out of her warm denim jeans and splashed happily into the cool clear water. She added her cries to those around her, rolling and diving and tumbling in sheer joy. All of a sudden a thought occurred to her. Maybe Pidgy would like to swim too! Water glistening on her skin, she hurried out of the water and up to Pete and the ponies.

"Pete!" she cried. "I want to take Pidgy swimming too. Can I?"

Pete considered this startling request for a moment and, not seeing what harm it could do, agreed. "O.K. Cindy, I guess it'll be all right. But we'd better go down to the other end of the pond. These kids might not like sharing their territory with a pony!"

Soggy wet as she was with her swim suit still dripping, Cindy jumped on the patient Pidgy who long ago had become used to doing things not generally asked of ponies. It was like the time Cindy had brought her into the house! Oh, but that's another story...

At the far end of Randall's Pond grew rushes and reeds and lily pads. And FROGS! Some sudden splashing announced that, their sunning interrupted, a few of these long-legged jumping jacks had made a swift departure to the pond's cool depths. When Cindy and Pete arrived, three round ripples, growing wider, were the only indication that there had been any action among the lily pads.

"Well, go ahead my little hoss-lovin' water fairy, let's see how Pidgy makes out as a sea horse,—or should I say 'pond pony'?" laughed Pete, rather proud of his witticism.

Cindy giggled. Never was anyone more fun than Pete. She thought the world of him.

Pidgy wasn't too sure she wanted to be a "pond pony" however, so she stood at the water's edge with her ears turned back and shook her heavy forelock in a negative manner.

"Use your heels!" called Pete.

Cindy did. And Pidgy sprang into action. Impatiently she thrashed the water with flying hoofs, sending it in a fine spray in all directions. Cindy used her heels again. This time the pony, finding this water business might be rather fun, gathered all four legs together and gave a mighty

leap. KER-SPLASH! She did a perfect "belly-flop" right into the lily pads. Miraculously Cindy stayed with her. She was soaking wet again as was Pidgy, but neither thought about that.

The water at this end of the pond was clear enough but full of all kinds of sub-surface greenery. At least it had been clear until Pidgy's launching. Now everything was churned into a brown-green murkiness. Cindy's strong young legs clung to her

pony's sodden sides as with little leaps resembling those of a carousel horse, Pidgy swam gaily amid the rushes and lily pads.

The pony had lifted the tip of her muzzle and all her front teeth showed. Watching all this, Pete roared with laughter. It struck him as the funniest sight he had ever seen. There were Cindy and Pidgy floating about in the towering rushes with a

whole convoy of lily pads behind them. Their long
stems had tangled in the pony's ample tail. And
when Pidgy looked up with that ridiculous smile on
her pony face, Pete laughed till his sides ached and
he had to get off Old Lew before he fell off. As for
Cindy, she was having the time of her young life.

Just then a frog, panic-stricken at the sudden
and fearful invasion of his home, leaped in a

tremendous arc to land with a loud SPLOP right on Pidgy's nose! He apparently thought it was a rock. That did it! With a terrific snort Pidgy rose out of the water like a rocket. The angle of take-off and the pony's slippery sides were too much for Cindy and she slid off into the convoy of lily pads. Pidgy headed for shore as if all of King Neptune's watery goblins were after her.

Seeing that Cindy had disentangled herself successfully from the clinging lily pads, Pete hurried to the water's edge to catch Pidgy before she could take flight and head for home at a sloshing gallop. Once on dry land again, and exceedingly thankful to be there, the wide-eyed little mare shook herself violently. Spray and fragments of pond plants flew in all directions. Pete was generously doused. Finally, panting and splashing, Cindy reached shore. She too was liberally decorated with pond souvenirs. A lily pad dangled from one dripping braid and pieces of greenery clung to her arms and

legs. Like Pidgy she was a sight. Unable to contain himself Pete burst into uproarious laughter all over again. It was all just too funny! The little girl and her pony looked as though they had been swimming the Amazon River for a month!

Caught up by Pete's infectious laughter and always ready to see the humor in any situation, Cindy began to giggle. It was a very damp giggle at first but impelled by Pete's thundering mirth she, too, was soon shaking with laughter. Only poor Pidgy, wet and disheveled with an ever so tiny fragment of lily pad still caught in her tail, did not share in the gaiety. She thought the whole episode the height of foolishness and firmly resolved it would be a long hot day before she'd be a party to such a display of nonsensical goings-on again. At least that was how she looked!

"Pidgy disapproves," announced Pete still laughing but noting the pony's readable expression. "Probably won't talk to you all the way home!" And he roared with laughter all over again. Then he sobered. "Speaking of going home, we'd better! I promised your mother I'd have you back by 4:00 and it's almost that now!"

At that Cindy, her youthful spirits soaring, made a flying leap onto Pidgy's back. She landed with a loud SQUISH! Pete swung up on Old Lew who, with reins dangling, had been placidly chewing grass during the whole show. Trustworthy, that was Lew.

Most of the swimmers had gone when Pete and Cindy rode back along the shore of Randall's Pond. The raft looked desolate without the usual number of glistening bodies sprawled on it. Pete put Old Lew into a slow canter as they neared the trail. Cindy's blue jeans were looped loosely around her waist and they fluttered in the breeze. Pidgy's drying tail flapped noisily behind her. Thus they hurried through the shadowy woods toward home.

The summer days flew by as if on golden, winged hoofs and soon September came. School again! Now Cindy's jaunts were limited to quick rides on familiar trails, and she did not get over to Greenwood Farm as often.

PIDGY'S MISSING!

With approaching cool weather Pidgy's coat began to thicken, once more heralding winter. Her "teddy bear" appearance was returning with the last of the warm days. Long hairs grew on her underjaws and curled around the back of her knees. She began to look more roly poly than ever.

In the haze of autumn twilights, Cindy relived the bright summer days just past. Often after a short ride she would come home deep in thought. The fine horses of her dreams did not change with the season. Their coats remained shining silk. No ugly long hair appeared to spoil their beauty. The cooler days made them leap and prance even more than before, snorting jets of steam from fiery nostrils . . . Because of her blue ribbon, Pidgy sometimes "shared their range" where ponies never were before. Cindy would imagine little round Pidgy with the raggedy coat standing near and peeking around a tall glossy Thoroughbred. And she would smile, remembering what the judge at the horse show had said to her, "Time enough for that, young lady, time enough for that." At least she had Pidgy. And Pidgy had won a BLUE RIBBON!

Autumn came and was a blaze of color before the cold wind. Then with icy fingers winter snatched the bright leaves. The trees, transformed, were stark and bare. Then the snow came and rides meant bundling up in heavy clothing, seeing your breath on icy mornings, rosy cheeks and red noses and cold fingers. It meant dreams of horses plunging in powdery snow. It meant finding Pidgy snorty and full of play. And it meant that summer was a distant thing . . . January, February, March, April . . . Like a revolving top time spun swiftly away.

Then soon winter's siege was broken. The spring sun warmed the waiting earth. All the icy defenses melted and nourished growing things.

The peepers sang again in the brook under the willows. Hearing them one evening, Cindy dreamed of the Phantom of the Mist. On the night of the new moon in early May, she waited by the pasture fence hoping he might return. She strained her eyes into the mist above the brook as it floated silently through the willows. She listened for the throbbing hoof-beats. But the peepers made the only sound and the rising mist was the only movement in the willows. The Phantom did not appear.

∪ ∪ ∪

Early one morning in late May as Cindy ran down the dew-covered path to feed Pidgy her morning oats, she stopped short in her tracks. The pasture gate was open! Pidgy was nowhere in sight. Cindy gasped in horrified disbelief. Then suddenly she thought, the feed box! She's raiding the feed box! And she's so fat now she'll explode! Breathlessly

109

Cindy ran into the barn. Silence. She looked into the feed room. It was empty! She ran back out to the pasture. Maybe Pidgy was in the far corner. But the pasture was empty. Pidgy had disappeared.

On shaking legs Cindy raced to the house. She burst into the kitchen screaming, "Mother, Daddy, Pidgy's gone, Pidgy's gone! The pasture gate's open, she's gone! The barn's empty, too!"

Mr. and Mrs. Sawyer exchanged worried glances.

"Where could she have gone, Mom, where?" cried Cindy, tears brimming in her eyes. "Someone's stolen Pidgy; taken her away!" The tears could be held back no longer. They streamed down poor Cindy's flushed face in salty twin rivers.

"We'll find her, honey, don't cry!" soothed her mother.

"She must have been working on that latch for days, our little Miss Houdini. Probably over in Wilson's garden now, nibbling on his asparagus!" Mr. Sawyer tried humor to check Cindy's tears, but without success.

"Oh, Daddy, we've got to find her!" sobbed Cindy. "Maybe something awful's happened to her. I'm going to call Pete!" And she made a dash for the telephone.

"Wait, wait, Cindy! Don't bother Pete. Not yet, anyway. Let's check around here first before we get hysterical," said Mr. Sawyer.

"But where, Daddy?" sobbed Cindy.

"We can ask the neighbors. Maybe someone's seen her."

All morning Mr. Sawyer and his tearful young daughter inquired around the village about the pony. But no one had seen Pidgy. In the afternoon Cindy suggested trying Alice's, hoping the pony might have wandered over there. Still no luck. Mr. Sawyer finally called Pete but the young man hadn't seen the plucky little pony either. Pidgy appeared to be really lost.

111

At supper that night, Cindy refused to eat. She just couldn't. How could she eat when Pidgy might be far away and suffering some horrible fate? Finally, knowing it was useless to coax her, Mrs. Sawyer excused her from the table. Cindy opened the kitchen door and went out into the cool spring twilight. When the door had closed behind her small sad figure, Mrs. Sawyer said with a sigh. "We have to find Pidgy, and soon!"

"Maybe Pete will call..." Mr. Sawyer pushed away from the table, too. He didn't feel much like eating, either.

Out by the pasture fence Cindy stared into the darkness. It just didn't seem possible that Pidgy was gone, really gone. She called softly hoping that maybe after all the pony had come home to get her supper and was out there in the shadows now.

"Pidgy, Pidgy, come on Pidge, your oats are here," she called in a choked voice.

Only silence, heavy as her heart, answered her. Even the peepers were still. There was no moon and no mist; just empty darkness. And somewhere Pidgy was out in it, alone and hungry.

"Oh, Pidgy, Pidgy," whispered Cindy and she put her hot face against the top rail of the fence and sobbed; great wracking sobs, heartrending to hear. "If you'll only come back Pidgy, I'll never care about dream horses again. They've all gone, Pidgy, I don't see them at all now, not at all. They were just dreams, Pidge. You're alive. I can touch you and ride you and really hear you nicker to me. Oh, Pidgy, come back, come back." And Cindy wept as if her heart would break.

All the thoughts of summer days with the pony flashed into her sorrowing mind. "Remember the horse show and the silly little boy with the lollypop and remember how you showed them all by winning the Blue; remember the rides with Pete and swimming in Randall's Pond? How funny you looked with lily pads dangling from your tail . . . Pidgy, Pidgy, come home, come home. I'll never say you're fat and fuzzy and funny any more. I love you, Pidgy, I do, I do." Her tears splashed softly on the rough top rail of the fence and fell to the grass.

Mr. Sawyer crossed the lawn from the house. He could hear Cindy crying bitterly in the darkness. He did not like the sound. His child was suffering real grief. He had never realized how much the pony actually meant to her. Suppose something should happen to Pidgy? Mr. Sawyer cast this terrible thought from his mind almost as fast as it had appeared. Nothing would happen. It couldn't. He prayed fervently.

"Don't cry like that, Cindy. Everything will be all right. We'll find her, honey, we're sure to. Just don't cry so hard." Mr. Sawyer put his arms around her. He felt very helpless in the face of her grief. "I'll go in and call Pete again," he said. "Maybe there's some news." Gently and slowly he led his little daughter back to the house.

With some difficulty Mrs. Sawyer put the tired and heartbroken Cindy to bed. Luckily the little girl fell at once into a deep sleep of exhaustion.

As soon as Cindy was in bed, Mr. Sawyer called Pete. "Any luck, Pete? Did you find Pidgy?" he asked anxiously.

"No, Mr. Sawyer. I'll let you know right away if I find her. How is Cindy?"

"She's taking it pretty hard, Pete. Cried her eyes out after supper."

"She thinks a lot more of that pony than she ever let on; more than she would even admit to herself, I bet," Pete said. His voice sounded tired.

"Well, call us, Pete, if there's any news."

"Oh, I will, I will, Mr. Sawyer. Don't you worry, though, everything'll be O.K." Pete assured him.

"Goodnight, then."

"Goodnight."

Mr. Sawyer hung up. "We'll just have to wait and hope," he said to his wife who was tiptoeing downstairs. "Cindy asleep?"

"Yes, thank goodness. It's been a very hard day for her—for all of us," she added.

PIDGY'S SURPRISE

It was early the next morning when the telephone jangled in the Sawyer home. Aroused at once by the shrill sound, Mr. Sawyer leaped from bed and, struggling into his robe, hurried downstairs—two steps at a time—to answer it.

"Hello—this Pete?" he shouted into the receiver.

"Mr. Sawyer? Yes, Pete. Mr. Sawyer, she's here. Tell Cindy to come!" Pete was so excited he was almost incoherent.

"You found Pidgy?" asked Mr. Sawyer, the excitement in his voice obvious.

"Yes, I found her a few minutes ago."

"How is she?"

"Just fine, Mr. Sawyer, just fine. And Mr. Sawyer?"

"Yes, Pete?"

"Tell Cindy that Pidgy has a big surprise for her!"

"A surprise? What are you talking about?"

"You'll have to see for yourself!"

"We'll be out there as soon as we can, Pete, right away, in fact!" Almost before he had slammed down the receiver, Mr. Sawyer called, "Janet, Cindy, everybody up! Pidgy's found! She's at Greenwood Farm! She's fine!"

Cindy came running down the stairs, wide awake and hardly able to contain herself. "Pidgy, Pidgy! She's safe! Where did you say she is, Daddy? Where?"

"At Greenwood Farm. Hurry now and get dressed. She's probably anxious to get home."

The car bumped along the dirt road to Greenwood Farm, its breakneck speed ridiculous for the hills and curves of the route.

"Cindy, sit still, stop fidgeting, we're almost there," exclaimed Mrs. Sawyer. "Just a few minutes more."

"Pidgy's all right, isn't she, Daddy?" asked Cindy for the hundredth time since Pete's call. "You're sure she's all right?"

"Yes, honey, Pidgy's just fine. Don't worry."

A few minutes later the Sawyer's car sped through the gateway to Greenwood Farm. Pete dashed out to meet them, his face glowing with happiness and relief. Cindy leaped out almost before the car had stopped. "Pete, oh, Pete, take me to Pidgy! Where is she?"

"Easy there, easy," laughed Pete, grabbing Cindy's arm. "Calm down."

"Where is she?"

"In the broodmare pasture, honey. Go ahead."

Cindy's legs flew as she ran down the lane to the pasture beyond the paddocks. She scrambled over the white paneled fence and hurried across the meadows toward a group of horses. At first she didn't see her pony. Then a rangy chestnut moved away. And there was Pidgy—AND!!! Cindy stopped dead in her tracks. Standing on long, trembly legs stood a tiny foal. It was much too small to belong to

one of the Thoroughbreds. IT WAS PIDGY'S! Cindy could hardly believe what she saw. Shivers ran up and down her spine and her eyes filled with excited tears. A foal, Pidgy's foal! It couldn't be true!

Pidgy pricked her ears and nickered, almost as though assuring her young mistress it was true. Quite true! Cindy walked up to the pony and the tiny foal. "Oh, Pidgy, I'm so glad to see you. I was so worried. And Pidgy, your baby, he's beautiful!" The little colt pricked his fuzzy ears and took a shaky step toward Cindy. His ruffled coat was a sort of pale silvery gray and his short silky mane and

tail were white. Suddenly he moved. Taking a few
more shaky steps he began to walk away from his
dam. At each step he felt stronger. Soon he began to
trot, his short curly tail straight out behind him.
Cindy was fascinated. She watched as though hyp-
notized. The little foal put on quite a show. When
the Sawyers and Pete came upon the scene he was
trying to convince his mother to play hide and seek
among the Thoroughbred mares. Pidgy whinnied
loudly calling him back. He came at a rickety run.
Everyone laughed. Then he stopped short and
stared at them with wide, wild eyes.

"Oh, Pete, isn't he wonderful?" cried Cindy all in one breath.

Pete nodded.

Mr. and Mrs. Sawyer looked at each other with confused expressions. "How?" they asked together.

"Remember last year, when Pidgy escaped and we found her in the pasture with our pony stallion?" asked Pete.

Mr. and Mrs. Sawyer both smiled.

He's just like the Phantom of the Mist, only younger and smaller, thought Cindy to herself. Now I can raise horses like the Phantom—only they'll be PONIES! "I'll raise them in miniature!" she cried out loud.

"What on earth are you talking about, Cindy?" asked the child's mother.

"Phantoms!" cried Cindy.

"Phantoms?" echoed the Sawyers and Pete in amazement. "What in the world—"

"PONIES—wild 'n' beautiful 'n' spirited PONIES—like the Phantom of the Mist!" explained Cindy patiently.

Since they'd never heard about the Phantom of the Mist, Pete and the Sawyers couldn't quite understand what Cindy meant.

"I'm GOING TO RAISE PONIES!" shouted Cindy.

120

At this announcement Mr. Sawyer pushed back his hat and scratched his head. All year he had been hearing nothing but horses, horses, horses and now—"Children!" he murmured.

"No, dear," said Mrs. Sawyer quietly. "You mean PONIES!"

∪ ∪ ∪
GLOSSARY

A

admonished criticized or scolded

B

bay having a brown body and black points

be a party to such a display to participate in something

blue roan having a black head, mane, tail and legs with a body that is gray which does not lighten with age

C

canter a smooth, three-beat gait that is faster than a trot but slower than a gallop

chestnut reddish brown

colt a young male horse

D

dam a mother horse

dappled having spots or patches of lighter color

dejection sadness

disdainful filled with disgust or dislike toward another

dun having a light golden body and black points

F

filly a young female horse

firm seat the ability of a rider to easily stay in the saddle or display good riding form

G

gaiety happiness

gaily happily

gait the movements of a horse including the walk, trot, canter, and gallop

H

haughtily with self-importance or arrogance

J

jangled rang; made a metallic-sounding noise

jaunt short trip

jiggly bouncy

jodhpurs riding pants

K

keep her chin up keep her spirits up

L

lead the position, at the canter, during which the inner front leg (the front leg closest to the center of the ring) is ahead of the other front leg

liberally generously

lisped mispronounced the *s* or *z* sounds as *th*

M

mirth happiness

mopped wiped the forehead (or other body part) to remove sweat

mused thought about

P

palomino having a yellow or golden hide and light colored points

piebald having a black hide and white spots

pinto having two colors: white and spots of either brown, black, gray, etc. where each spot is larger than 2 inches

placidly calmly

prance to walk with lively, bouncy action

public address system electronic devices and loudspeakers, such as those used at a horse show, that allow exhibitors to hear the announcer

R

rangy thin with long legs

S

sassily rudely; with bad manners

sire a father horse

soft hands the ability to ride in a manner that is forgiving and gentle to a horse's mouth

S.P.C.A. Society for the Prevention of Cruelty to Animals; an organization dedicated to the kind treatment of animals

T

trellis　a structure, made of interwoven wood or other material, that supports climbing plants

trot　a two-beat diagonal gait that is faster than a walk but slower than a canter

V

vigor　enormous strength and energy

village　small town

W

witticism　a joke or clever statement